Anxiety in Relationship for couples

Essential guide to make effective communication in love, overcome couple conflicts and build your life happy without therapy

[David Wallace Beck]

You agree to accept all risks of using the information presented inside this book.

You agree that by continuing to read this book, where appropriate and/or necessary, you shall consult a professional (including but not limited to your doctor, attorney, or financial advisor or such other advisor as needed) before using any of the suggested remedies, techniques, or information in this book.

Table of Contents

Introduction

Being anxious is an integral part of what being human entails. Sometimes we are worried about those facets of our lives that we most care for: our health; our ability to clothe and support ourselves and our family; and our capacity to be linked and respected by others. Anxiety allows us to wake up in the morning intensively motivated to abandon our comfort zone.

Anxiety is a mental condition that can work for us as well as against us. It's something that we all share in common, but where we also vary is how we interpret these feelings of anticipation and how we react to it. Our situations in life, our culture and our attitudes can all be variables such that the thrilling rollercoaster experience of one person can leave another person in abject anxiety. Feeling anxious isn't a symptom of disappointment, and there are occasions when it's necessary to ask people around us or practitioners for support. However, as we come to a deeper understanding of anxiety, there is more we should do as people and take action to reduce its control on us and to learn to accept our full range of feelings without allowing it to overtake us.

Chapter 1: Anxiety

What Is Anxiety

Anxiety has many names, including common anxiety, social anxiety, and post-traumatic stress disorders; these three are only a couple! A person with an anxiety disorder may frequently experience panic attacks or anxiety attacks that can be very serious and life-changing.

When is an attack of anxiety? An anxiety disorder is a mental condition in which one or more symptoms may be felt, often very severe and frightening. Some of the common signs of an anxiety attack include adrenaline, sweaty hands, weak legs that can't hold you, fear of imminent death, hyperventilation, suffocating sensation, arms, and legs numbness, blurry sight and much more. You may feel like you will die during an anxiety attack. It's an intense feeling of helplessness and anxiety that makes you believe you've just been running a marathon. It hurts you physically and mentally, and after a panic attack, it is no uncommon for anyone to sleep for a long time.

The frequency of anxiety disorders will vary from time to time each day, depending on the intensity of the attack and whether it is handled or not. Panic attacks take a lot from you, and sometimes you believe life will never change. Several factors can lead to an anxiety attack and are typically related to fear or change. Nonetheless, it's not uncommon if someone has an anxiety disorder and doesn't know why.

There are also therapies available for people with anxiety. Those include drugs such as narcotics against anxiety, psychotherapy, and natural treatments, including other plants or a change of diet. No matter what kind of anxiety you have, medication is available to seek.

Many ordinary people suffer from anxiety or claim that they frequently suffer from anxiety during conversations. Yet, what is fear? What is the fear? Anxiety is a term used in various illnesses that can become physical manifestations triggered by stressed, anxious, and worrying conditions. There are various types of anxiety where you can be mild and distracted by more serious symptoms that cause physical and mental health issues.

Anxiety typically arises when someone is faced with something beyond their comfort zone, and thus many challenging situations can occur. For instance, if you were to take a test, attend an interview, or speak. It affects people in many ways as for others, these conditions can be considered natural, but for many others, they can affect the whole life, such as being unable to sleep, making mistakes, or failing to eat properly. In general, anxiety arises when the normal expectation exaggerates a reaction. Disorders of anxiety may be divided into more common groups. The most popular causes of anxiety are below.

G.A.D-A Generalized Anxiety Disorder Generalized Anxiety Disorder (G.A.D.) is a severe type of anxiety that is characterized by extreme long-term anxiety. These G.A.D. sufferers worry about all manner of problems. It can be family life, work-related issues, safety, money worries, but it can be difficult to identify their fears. Outsiders are also perceived as a bit superficial and overblown by this apprehension of what is generally expected in such circumstances. It can also be seen as unreasonable, as they can not concentrate and are too dismissive of the person who is having trouble addressing trivial yet distressing daily problems, such as social events, relationships, and work-related issues.

Post-traumatic stress disorder (PTSD) Post-traumatic stress disorder (PTSD) is anxiety triggered by an earlier, particularly distressing situation. There may be extreme cases, such as whether someone has been kidnapped or burgled in extremely serious cases like hostage situations, kidnapping, or the battle of a soldier. Post-traumatic stress disorder involves recalling the situation, which may cause discomfort when the situation is remembered

Understanding Anxiety

No matter how secure your partner is, the constant anxiety, frustrations, neediness, fears, and worries of the anxiously attached person will eventually seep into the relationship.

As they are more likely to pick dismissive or avoidant partners, there is another layer of issues added to the relationship interactions.

You must learn to understand how your insecure behaviours affect your partner, and other people you interact with.

In the romantic comedy 'How to lose a guy in 10 days,' a writer's best friend is going through 'yet another break-up' due to her neediness and clingy behaviour.

What follows is a hilarious albeit over the top exercise in how to drive someone away: the constant calling and leaving far too many messages, being overly close and intimate too soon, nagging and testing, the temper tantrums, going from loving to naked hatred in ten seconds, excessive neediness, and even fake couple's counseling.

For you partner to understand your needs, and what triggers you, you need to communicate openly and clearly. Similarly, you need to understand how these behaviours affect your partner, and what may be triggers for them.

Understand your own needs, and communicate them.

Consistency – as a perception of lack of safety is an extremely important trigger. Keep the relationship balanced, avoid highs and lows.

Communicate feelings and affection – regularly. Being told you are desirable and loved is important for reassurance. A text or call will do the trick.

Love language: you tend to give love the way you want to receive it, so it is important to understand your partner's love language to help them feel safe.

Reassurance in conflict – every fight is not about to end the relationship, but you need to be told this and reassured.

Never invalidate feelings – it reactivates the inner child.

Follow through – the little things matter a great deal, as it provides reassurance in the face of insecurity.

Understand how your partner perceives this.

Your partner will need patience, strong security, and self-esteem; otherwise you may trigger the following:

Nagging – feelings of never being able to do enough for you, being pressurized to do things he is not ready for.

Constant closeness – being smothered, need to move away

Jealousy – not being trusted

Impatience and anger – exasperation and irritability, loss of respect.

Acting out, driving your partner away – the perception that you are not available or not feeling affection.

Behavioural Differences Due To Anxiety

Unhealthy anxiety can have a big impact on your life. It will hinder you from doing the things you desire. When you are anxious, you get a feeling that your life is under the control of an external force. Anxiety is a negative, vicious circle which consumes you completely and can have an effect on your wellbeing, your relationship, your hobbies, and more. It feels difficult to break this anxiety, but the possibility exists. Anxiety often makes people assume that they are no longer in charge and cannot do anything about it. This isn't the case - you can learn to get your anxieties under control and find happiness.

Anxiety disorder occurs when you regularly feel disproportionate levels of worry, tension, or fear due to an emotional trigger. The ability to identify the reason behind a series of anxiety attacks is the key to successful treatment.

Environmental factors:

Elements within your surroundings can trigger anxiety. Worries and stress associated with a private relationship, job, school, or monetary difficulty can lead to anxiety disorder.

Genetics:

Research has shown that if any members of your family have dealt with anxiety disorder, there is high chance that you will experience anxiety as well.

Medical factors:

Different medical issues can lead to an anxiety disorder, such as the side effects of drugs, symptoms of a sickness, or stress from a difficult underlying medical condition. These conditions could lead to significant lifestyle changes like pain, restricted movement, and even emotional imbalance. It is worth noting that anxiety can be triggered by any of these problems.

Brain chemistry:

Experiences that are traumatizing or stressful can alter the structure and performance of the brain, making it react to certain triggers that may not have previously caused anxiety.

Relationships are amazing and very fulfilling with the opportunity for happiness, fun, interesting conversations, and exciting dates. They can, however, also be a major source of upheaval and worry. Your ability to identify the major sources of anxiety in your relationship will help you stay away from them, thus enhancing the balance and stability of your relationship.

I will now take you through some of the most common triggers of anxiety in your relationships and how to look out for them and control them.

What triggers anxiety the most is when you are vulnerable to another person. We yearn for safety and love in a relationship. If you have been hurt before, the fear of being hurt again can make you anxious.

Financial concerns of either partner is another cause of anxiety in relationships. Most times, people do not fully disclose their money related issues or financial strengths. They open up when a problem arises, and at this point it may be too late. It could be that you are not compatible with your partner when it comes to saving and spending money, or you do not even share the same money views with them. It is also easy for you to get carried away by love and close your eyes to the financial wherewithal of your partner. When real life expenses sets in and you seem to be carrying the brunt of them, anxiety sets in. Money in relationships is a constant.

Another root cause of anxiety in relationships is jealousy. Your inability to trust your partner could lead to jealousy. Jealousy is also as a result of a lack of confidence in yourself and your abilities coupled with low self-esteem. In order to overcome this, build up your self-esteem and begin to think very highly of yourself. The best way to eradicate jealousy is by building up your self-esteem.

Jealousy can reveal our greatest fears and insecurities, and this can quickly lead to an unhealthy and toxic atmosphere in your relationship. When you are jealous, you become overwhelmed and begin to imagine the worst.

The fear of being abandoned and the fear of rejection are also major causes of anxiety in relationships. Whatever insecurities you have are mirrored back to you by your partner. It is only normal to worry about these things, but instead of keeping the thoughts to yourself, speak them out loud and have a conversation about them with your partner. You have to develop a stronger identity and sense of self. You have to learn to be consciously aware of your state of mind and thought processes in order to keep all anxieties at bay. Most of the arguments you have with your partner over your family, work, social life, or money actually have some form of rejection as their roots. The underlying feeling and fear during these fights is that you will be rejected. For instance, if you are having a heated discussion about how much time your partner spends with his friends, it is actually about why they aren't spending that time with you?

Your ability to relax into your relationship will make you feel less rejected and no longer defensive. Be present in your relationship and have no negative thoughts.

You must deliberately set clear boundaries on the type of information that gets into your head. Work to stop unwanted information and behaviors from coming in and penetrating into your mind.

When anxiety comes knocking at your door, open the door for it, address it, look at it, then inhale deeply and close the door, knowing that you have armed yourself with all the information that you need. You do not have to welcome anxiety with open arms, but you can acknowledge that it's there.

Ongoing communication with an ex is another trigger for anxiety. Communications with an ex should be handled cautiously. This is because it can lead to great anxiety, anger, and eventually a breakup in your current relationship. If you have to communicate with your ex, you should explain why to your partner and ensure all communication is strictly platonic and transparent. If you do not have to communicate with your ex, do not do it.

Distance backed up with a lack of communication can hugely contribute to anxiety between you and your partner. When your partner is not physically available for a long period of time, it can be difficult to find assurance and thus anxiety sets in. Even if you talk on the phone and video call regularly, you can still feel a void in your heart. In situations like this, you have to rely on the power of words to communicate your feelings with your partner. Feel free to tell your partner what you need from them, express yourself, and talk about any insecurities you may be going through. By so doing, your partner will be able to address this and reassure you of their love and commitment.

Another major cause of anxiety is doubt. It can be weakening to question every move and action of your partner, wondering if you made the right decision or what next steps you should or should not take. If you are in great doubt, begin to make a conscious effort to release yourself and set yourself free from doubt. Take your mind off every question that makes you doubt your relationship or your partner. Just take a deep breathe, calm down, and revel in your relationship. Make up your mind to just enjoy your relationship and your partner by allowing yourself the freedom of not having to make any decisions about your relationship for a period of time.

A major health challenge can also trigger anxiety in your relationship. You or your partner may be caught off guard by a diagnosis or medical scare. This may also stress you out and cause a great deal of anxiety within yourself. If you or your partner fall ill, anxiety will naturally set in. This health challenge may cause your partner to break down emotionally. You will have to be very patient and calm with them through this process. Provide all the support you can during this time and let them be assured of your unwavering love and commitment.

Understand Your Partner

Learning fear and what your partner is doing will help you to understand and assist the partner with some basic facts about anxiety. Psychologist Dave Carbonell, Ph.D. psychiatrist Dr. Helen Odessky, among others, suggested bearing these in mind:

- Anxiety is normal. Everybody's got it. It becomes a problem or disorder only if it is serious.

- Anxiety is a real problem, not a composite. It's a problem in mental health.

- Anxiety can be a crippling condition that prevents people from working and living a normal life.

- Anxiety causes people to experience flight and battle responses and worry about life-threatening issues, including whether a partner may cheat or leave.

- You can't "cure" or "fix." Anxiety

- Many people who have anxiety disorder wish they never had it. They are concerned that their anxiety is a burden for others.

- There are millions of people who have great relationships and are happy despite dealing with anxiety.

- Symptoms of anxiety, consistently or both may occur in waves. People with anxiety disorders or problems can have periods when they have no symptoms.

- Anxiety is not rational or logical. This causes people to worry about something, although there is no evidence that it is worth worrying. It also causes them to act irrationally sometimes. Your partner probably knows that.

- Anxiety is not a weakness.

Anxiety can be treated. Psychotherapy can alleviate symptoms and teach people how to treat them better

How To Eliminate Anxieties

A relationship is an awful thing to experience. This means you can't appreciate the magic of love, too worried that your partner will come out of it.

Ironically, your partner might want to put an end to all the negative energy that you worry about your relationship.

Luckily, you can do plenty to relax your mind and begin to change your outlook so that you can enjoy your relationship instead of living in constant stress.

Here are some easy ways to overcome your relationship anxiety:

1. Always remember that it's all going to be all right

If you are in the middle of a disintegrating relationship, it can easily feel like the end of the world. It can be extremely difficult to keep things in focus and see the light at the end of the tunnel when all those emotions rush.

It's as easy as to note that whatever happens, it's all alright. Think back. Think back. You have had heartbreak before, and you just got through it okay.

When you met your friend, you were perfectly fine, and life would go on after them if things ever go south.

Your life won't end if your relationship does, and being in a relationship isn't everything and not everything. A friendship can be fantastic, but it never determines you.

If somebody doesn't want to be with you, you can't do anything about it. You deserve to be with someone who moves heaven and earth.

When panic begins to rise, just murmur to yourself that all is all right. If you say it to yourself enough, you will start to believe it sooner or later.

However, the less you fear the end of the relationship, the more you can relax and enjoy it at the moment.

2.Discuss how you feel with your partner

A lack of communication or miscommunications also causes anxiety about relationships, so it's best to talk with your partner proactively.

If you plan to see each other, be the one to look for concrete details, like when and where. And this does not mean that you always have to decide (though you want to share this responsibility), it does mean that you are the organizer in your relationship.

You could say that it's just an extension of being too controlled, but it's not. You don't drive any small thing by yourself, but you are talking about flying.

If your relationship is more established but still anxious, talk from a place of honesty and openness to your partner.

Explain how you feel and remind them it's not they, but your past experiences. Try to provide examples of situations that are difficult for you and how they can alleviate your fears.

If the relationship is serious, you will want to do what you can to provide you with peace of mind.

It may also help you to express your feelings more pityingly if your anxieties cause you to do something that upsets them. You will know that what you say (or do) not necessarily mean all the time and that it can help you overcome your feelings by not adding fuel to the fire.

So asking your partner about your anxiety will actually make you feel better. In this regard, you will feel like a weight is lifted from your shoulders, and you're confident that they don't go anywhere if they react positively and with love.

3. Build your independence

If you're in love, you may feel that you're happy to live in your partner's pocket if you can, but losing yourself in your relationship is sure to boost your anxiety about your relationship.

If you just start defining yourself in terms of your relationship, you put too much pressure on it to be successful in the long term. Who would you be, after all, if you'd break up?

Make sure you do things consciously for yourself and keep a life apart from your partner. Try to retain the things that make you special, perhaps because your partner was first drawn to you.

Your companion is not your' other half,' and they are not finished you. You are fine and complete as you are. It's wonderful to be in a relationship, but not important to your happiness.

4.Stop analyzing your every move consciously

People comment throwaway. You don't ponder every word you say or evaluate how your nervous mind can view every text message you send. You should, therefore, not allow the little stuff to influence your state of mind.

5.Note that you control your mind, and it doesn't control you

You're not at your mind's mercy. You have the power to guide, shape, and train it. You may still experience fear once you've realized this, but you can recognize it for what it is and allow it, rather than allow it to consume you and guide your behavior.

Chapter 2: Insecurity

What Is Insecurity In Relationship

Insecurity is the tendency to lack any feeling of confidence or certainty in oneself. We all feel insecure at one time or another. Insecurity can be attached to all aspects of life. The most common insecurities we have are about our looks, jobs, and love life. Most people are capable of resolving their insecurity before it leaves a deeper impact in their lives. Some go through therapy, others can recognize it and deal with it on their own, but many people won't recognize insecurity and will confuse it with other negative feelings, such as jealousy. Helplessness and inadequacy are common feelings for insecure people. Because of these feelings, they are incapable of attending to common daily tasks or even form long-lasting, healthy relationships. People who feel insecure will often lack the ability to fit in society and think their actions and thoughts are constantly being judged by peers. They also believe they aren't worthy of acceptance or success. These beliefs will stop them from trying to achieve more. They will often be stuck in unsatisfying job positions without any motivation to go forward and work on receiving a promotion. They will lack the will to learn, work on themselves, thinking that there is no point as they will never be good enough. Even their love life suffers, probably the most. An insecure person will constantly crave a partner's validation. When he gets it, he will choose not to believe it or believe it's sincere.

In a small amount, insecurity in a relationship can be good as it gets you to work harder and devote yourself more to that relationship. Small jealousy acts can be seen as sweet and make us value our partner more. But the trick is in the small amount of insecurity, if it grows to be pathological, it will most certainly influence the relationship in the most negative way. It will, if not treated, eventually lead to a break-up. The destruction of a relationship caused by one person's insecurities is always very dramatic and painful for both sides. It will leave marks on both partners, deepening insecurities that already exist, or creating other anxieties related to relationships.

Knowing how your insecurities influence the relationship is important. By recognizing the signs of disaster your insecurity is creating, you will acknowledge its existence and can start working on yourself.

We all cope with negative thoughts about our relationships from time to time, and that's normal. We are all somewhat possessive of our partners. It gets really tricky when we start to act on those negative thoughts; when we manifest negative thoughts into negative actions. This is what ruins most relationships. This usually doesn't happen overnight, it takes time and it happens in stages. This is why it's hard for people to recognize the actions of their insecurities.

Getting Over Relationship Insecurity

Sometimes it is normal that you feel insecure, especially if you care about your partner when you are in a relationship. Envy is always nice and can make the relationship even more enjoyable and exciting. Yet, what if this insecurity becomes deeper and more overwhelming?

The common theory of cause for envy is that people are afraid of sexual dishonesty. Women are more concerned about emotional unfaithfulness because they are committed to their children's survival and want their husbands to love, care for and protect their children. Today more than ever, people are afraid that they will lose someone they love, that they are ignored, not remembered, not appreciated and not worried about. Such feelings of loss are common. Nonetheless, they are again partly derived from unsafe conditions when ideas and feelings of envy are extreme. Security increases as apprehension increases. Here are some useful solutions if you get insecure too much:

Don't Act on Your Feelings: The sensation of envy or other senses is not the problem; when you start to behave and allow the envy, the real problem starts. You can feel it, but you don't have to act. Be mindful that your better half is someone who regularly interacts with the world around you. This world includes people who are sexually wanted, but that doesn't mean they can betray you. Because of one thing or the other, they are closely linked to you. When you stop acting on your insecure feelings, you take charge of your emotions and then change your thought, wisdom and decisions.

Calm Down and Stay Vulnerable: It has a range. The best thing to do is to open your heart and welcome everything that comes and get calm again. George R. R. Martin once told me, "The more satisfied you are, the more people desire you. Indeed, this isn't easy, but you must be able to take on the unexpected and deal with what is beyond your control. Remember, if you want to love, you must be calm.

Softly express Your Insecurity: If you feel like your partner is doing something that makes you angry, you can express how you feel and respectfully talk to them. And with laughter, friendship and respect, you will know how to best convey it. If you're funny, you might joke how crazy you are while your partner is looking at someone else. Talk to them as they take the stare away from the subject and give the message. If you are patient and you know that they're never going to betray you, you should tell them that you love them a lot. And if you're honest, tell them you're confident in them, but you can't control your emotions, and you should be worried about what they feel.

Appreciate Yourself: Self-esteem and fear are a significant cause for envy amongst many people. Building your own self-esteem will ease your worries about other people. There is one reason why you enjoyed being in love and were first and foremost in love with your partner, but it's better if you love yourself first. If you feel insecure next time, mind that your partner is there because they want to be with you for your good qualities.

Heal Your Wounds: People also seem insecure because of past relationships. You might have been hurt, and they might have cheated on you. You have to look past your old relationships and know that you're in a new one.

The person you're in is not your former partner. Knowing the origins, reasons and motivations behind your insecurity is an important consideration for a healthy relationship and personal growth. If you feel vulnerable, try to heal your old wounds by being more resilient and deliberate, so that your present and your future are not affected by your past.

Trust your Partner: You have to have faith in your partner, and you have no other choice if you want a healthy, successful connection. You will let the insecurity go because your partner shouldn't be abused by anyone. There is no mistake in getting control, but it's difficult to try to manage something you don't know. Act cautiously, even though you are nervous.

Trust Yourself: The only thing you can do is trust yourself. You're sure you can love profoundly without any regret. Be sure that your passion for love does not float away in your relationship. It's not easy, but when you trust, you have faith in everything. You can live with the most difficult situation, such as a divorce or rejection.

In other words, insecurity can be harmful and can poison any romantic relations. You're more confident in building your partnership and building trust by implementing the above suggestions and strategies until you're satisfied.

Jealousy In Marriage: Why It Happens And Dealing With It

The typical transformative explanation for jealousy is that males fear sex-related cheating as they want to be sure that their offspring is theirs. Females are a lot more interested in emotional extramarital relations because they are interested in their youngsters' survival and also wish to see to it that their partner supports their kids, offer and shield them.

Today more than ever before, individuals are afraid of being rejected, declined, not being loved, and also bother with shedding people they take care of. These feelings of loss are all-natural. Yet, once again, when believed as well as feelings of jealousy are severe, they stem partially as a result of insecurities. When they are afraid lessens, so does jealousy.

If you experience jealousy often, below are some approaches that will assist you out:

1. Do not Act Upon Your Sensations

It is difficult not to act the means you are feeling. The feeling of jealousy or any other sensations is not the issue; the genuine difficulty begins when you start working upon that jealousy and let it consume you. You can feel the excitement, yet do not have to act upon it. Remember that your spouse is a human being that is actively communicating with the world around him/her. That globe has individuals of sex that they sexually like; however, that does not imply that they will cheat on you with them. There is a reason that they remain in an intimate connection with you. If they intended to date other people, they would undoubtedly have done so. So, the next time you feel jealous, approve the sensations, yet transform the method you think of the circumstance and also be reasonable as well as sensible.

2. Calm Down as well as Remain Vulnerable

To enjoy is to be susceptible. George R.R. Martin stated it most beautiful "The more people you will love, the weaker you will be." What you should do is to open your heart to your companion, depend on whatever comes, and also keep calm. Yes, it is challenging, but you require to be happy to approve what is past your control and trust fund yourself to handle the unknown. Keep in mind; you remain in the partnership since you decide to enjoy it. It is a choice you make to like your partner and, at the same time, approve the risks with no agitations or jealousy.

3. Express Your Jealousy in A Soft Method

If you feel that your companion is doing something that is making you envious, you can share exactly how you feel as well as talk with them in a mature means. You can likewise connect it with wit, diplomacy, or straight as long as it is considerate. If you are amusing, you can joke concerning exactly how remarkably envious you are when your partner focuses on somebody else. Laugh with them as you claim this because it will certainly take the pressure off the topic and will get the message throughout. When you are diplomatic, you can let them understand that you like them a whole lot and know that they can never cheat on you. And if you are straight, simply tell them that you trust them, yet can not manage your feelings and also desire them to consider just how you feel.

4. Value Yourself

Among the primary reasons why people get envious is that they have low self-esteem and insecurity problems. They tend to think that they are unsatisfactory, their companion will certainly understand this, and also will leave them for somebody else. You require to recognize that there is a reason that your partner liked you to begin with and even got together with you. If you need some reaffirmation or appreciation, do not think twice to ask for that too (within reason, of course). The next time you feel envious, keep in mind that your companion is with you since they intend to be with you because of your favorable qualities.

5. Heal Your Injuries

People often tend to act envious because of previous connections as well. You might have been injured before as well as they could have ripped off on you. You need to relocate beyond your past and also realize that you run out that partnership and even in a new one. The person that you are with is not your ex-partner. Understanding the roots, causes, and also reasons for your jealousy is an essential part of individual growth and preserving a healthy partnership.

6. Trust fund Your Companion

You must trust your companion because you have no other choice if you want to have a delighted and active connection. No person can control your companion, and also you need to allow jealousy to go. Having some control is not a negative point, yet attempting to manage somebody for things over which you have no control, is problematic. Act lovingly despite sensations of jealousy you experience.

7. Trust fund Yourself

The best point that you can do is count on yourself. Count on yourself that you can love deeply as well as with no regrets. Trust fund on your own that your love will act like the anchor that will avoid your relationship from floating away. This is difficult, yet eventually, when you trust on your own, you trust whatever comes. You feel the confidence that you will be able to take care of also one of the most challenging situations, consisting of a breakup or denial.

Finally, jealousy may be destructive and also serves as a poison in intimate connections. If you comply with the above tips as well as methods when feeling jealous, you will undoubtedly remain in a far better placement to develop your partnership and also grow the depend on.

How To Overcome Insecurities In Your Relationship

We're both grappling with anxiety at some stage or another; it's a natural way to try to gauge whether our plans are going to be productive or end terribly for us. In the case of having to determine whether or not to climb a major canyon on a motorbike, this is a really good assessment. Yet being too inexperienced in real life to attempt even minor things, such as being honest with partners, limits your ability to enjoy the time you have on Earth. Life is always evolving, and everything that is secure today can be destroyed or gone tomorrow. So, if you make yourself stronger, you will still restore, conquer, and step on with your own will, and find joy everywhere you go.

Adjusting your view

Process to be realistic. If you feel like you can't do it, take a step out of yourself for a moment and pretend you're a totally different guy. Talk of what you're about to tell someone else about your case. For example, if you're worried about going to a party where you don't know a lot of people or you're interviewing for a new job, talk of the advice you'd give a person in a similar circumstance. When you look at it this way, you will find that there is little to be afraid of and that you will excel when you set your mind to it.

Write down your doubts, please. Write down all the stuff you're thinking about, and all the things that make you feel like you can't do it. Read them over and ask yourself how many of them are logical and how many are simply the result of cynical thought. Take the time to truly talk about what's at the heart of your fears — whether it's making a fool of yourself, deceiving your friends, or not getting the life you deserve. See how many of your concerns you can tackle, and how many constructive ideas you can dream about for all the issues you're worried about.

It's completely normal to be scared of disappointment or of looking terrible. From time to time, everybody has these worries. It's normal, though, to be so afraid that you feel like you can't do a single thing.

Remember all the success you've achieved. Instead of dwelling on all the moments you humiliated yourself, missed something, or simply looked dumb, you should take a long, hard look at all the moments you did pretty well. Think of the achievements you've had in college, the wonderful connections you've built, or all the occasional moments that you've made a group of people crack up because of your sense of humor. The more days you recall, the more confidence you may have that you will get more of them in the future. It might be useful to write down the wish of your achievements when they happen. Hold a log of accomplishment at your desk and fill it with proud successes and happy memories. When you are powerless to do something and are like you can't do something right, you can look at your list and know what an amazing, talented person you are.

Tell yourself, "What's the worst thing that could happen?" and be frank about your answer. If you have a new haircut and a few people don't like it, it's impossible to destroy the planet. When you really dislike it, so guess what—-the hair regrows. Don't let these dumb fears deter you from doing anything new. When you know that the worst isn't that bad, you're more likely to be adventurous and take chances.

If you can't say when your comments stop being rational and start being crazy, try and run it by someone you know to be receptive to. They should be able to tell you whether or not the worst-case situation is realistic.

Now, ask yourself, "What's the best thing that might happen?" It's something dangerous people don't do nearly enough. Let's say you're worried about having a first date with someone you're matched up with. The best thing that can happen is that you and the person hit it off and continue a positive and fulfilling relationship. Isn't this worth going back on a second date? While the perfect thing is not necessarily going to happen, getting it on the table will help you handle new challenges with a good outlook.

Before you set out to try something different, you can always write down the best thing that can happen, or the top three things that can happen, and they're fresh on your head when the time comes.

Remember your positive characteristics

To protect yourself, you have to keep your great qualities at the bleeding edge of your psyche. Create a list of all the things you enjoy about yourself, from your friendliness to your intellect, and keep it at the forefront of your mind while you interact with someone else. Insecure people prefer to concentrate more on the bad aspects of themselves, which causes them to feel uncomfortable with who they are.

When focusing only on the negative things that are different from yourself, you dwell on them and forget the positive qualities. If you've been harsh on yourself for a long time, it can be hard to think about anything worth it at all.

Practice positive self-talking. It's particularly hard to hear negative self-talk if you've been doing it for a long time. If you're constantly reminding yourself that you're a loser, a disappointment, or that you can't do something good, you're expected to feel that way forever. Instead, focus on reminding yourself good thoughts about yourself, and you're more able to tackle new challenges with a balanced attitude and a willingness to do better.

A good practice to make you feel confident with constructive self-talk and to reel in self-abuse is to tell yourself two really nice things about yourself with every bad one. They don't have to be connected to it.

For e.g., if you burn your tongue because you didn't wait long enough for your coffee to cool down and yell, "Idiot! That was a dumb mistake" to yourself, then you have to note, "But I play tennis pretty well, and I have a nice sense of humor." It might sound weird, but you're changing your attitude when you applaud yourself.

Ask why you say no to yourself. Start answering yes more often than not. Instead of asking yourself all the reasons that you want to say no to a new encounter, consider thinking over what could happen if you say yes. And if all of the responses aren't real, the yes situation might lead to new and unforeseen stuff. If you get a little injured when you say yes to a new experience, you will rebound and get a different experience under your belt than if you just said no. If nothing comes of it at all, you should be able to think that you are a kind of optimistic and outgoing person ready to try new things.

Say a distant friend of yours from your music class is contacting you and telling you they want to start a band, and they want you to join them. Your automatic response may be, "No way, I've never been to a band, and you certainly don't seem to know how to make a successful one — otherwise, I don't think of myself as a musician, and I don't have time with classes, and ..." In this way of thinking, before anything has gone anywhere, you've already shut yourself down and denied any exploration of the potential of the idea. You could get in contact with the friend and their families, have a fun opportunity out of it, and have a new story to share. Say yes to see where you're headed.

Unless you are uncertain about your relationship, try to follow any of the above steps. Often, seeking self-happiness is still going well. If you're a genuinely happier guy, odds are you're going to make certain people and your wife happier; that's why it's going to lead you to trust and away from fear.

Trust Your Partner

You have to trust your partner. Why would you share your life with somebody after you assume they're doing one thing wrong each time you switch your back? If you don't trust your partner to be trustworthy, honest, caring or anything, then you're not in a very sensible relationship. The most effective relationships begin with a deep trust, and though issues come back up (and they will!), the trust is robust enough to stay you along.

Chapter 3: Negative Thoughts

What Are Negative Thoughts In Relationships

Negative thoughts come from our core beliefs and as such they will never go away. There are people who always seem positive, and it is true they might be more positive than others, but that is due to their own system of core beliefs. There is no such person who doesn't have negative thoughts. We all are victims of our insecurities. They are either better in managing their responses to negative thoughts or their core beliefs are completely different. They might be the lucky ones who grew up in a safe, loving environment but if you ask them they, too, have insecurities and negative thoughts to some degree.

Effects Of Negative Thoughts

Negative thoughts are cognitive barriers that your relationships are dealing with. When you make progress and turn from insecurities-driven negative behaviors to those driven by your values, you will still find yourself dealing with negative thoughts. If you want to learn how to manage them in a way that won't hurt your relationship, you will have to understand what they are and how they work.

Negative thoughts may come as:

1. Predictions you make based on your core beliefs and past experiences. These may include rejection, abuse, failure, or abandonment. Predictions are not to be seen as premonitions; they are more expectations. We are so convinced that they are going to happen no matter what and our behavior is leading us into more situations that can cause these expectations to actually happen. This is why we call them predictions.

2. Memories of past situations, losses, and failures. We are prone to remember situations that hurt us much more than the ones that

are happy. This is due to our defense mechanisms being at work. We have to remember hurtful situations and experiences to avoid them in future.

3.   Negative judgments, that we have about us or the others. Negative judgment comes from insecurities, and it also reflects on others. In them, we see our own insecurities and we easily pass the judgment as a coping mechanism.

As you accepted your core beliefs as something that is constant, and you have no influence over, so should you do with negative thoughts. They come from core beliefs, and we cannot stop them. They will constantly pop up in our minds whether we try to stop them or we don't. The fight you would put in trying to think only positive is futile, there is no amount of strength that will help you achieve this. You may succeed in pushing away negative thoughts temporarily, but they will always come back. You need to accept that negative thoughts happen to everyone and are not controllable. Again, what is controllable is your reaction to them.

At all costs avoid coping behaviors such as drug use, alcohol, gambling, risky sex… These behaviors will numb you so you don't feel emotions that accompany negative thoughts, but you will never get rid of them. This behavior will only create more negative thoughts about yourself and it will spin you in enchanted circle of bad coping mechanisms.

Fear Of Abandonment

Many people grow up with worries around desertion. Some are tormented by these worries quite regularly throughout their lives. They fret they'll be declined by peers, partners, schools, business, or whole social circles. For numerous others, these concerns aren't fully realized until they participate in an enchanting relationship. Points will be accompanying efficiently, and all of an abrupt, they feel inundated with instability as well as the dread that their partner will undoubtedly distance themselves, disregard, or leave them. Everyone experiences this concern at different degrees.

The level to which an individual is confronted with this concern can form precisely how they live their lives and experience their partnerships. However, there are several ways for people to develop even more protection within themselves and also conquer their fear of abandonment. They can begin by understanding where this fear comes from. Exactly how and also why does it establish? How does it impact me in my present life? What are the techniques for dealing with the anxiety that develops? How can I improve a lot more strength and experience less be afraid around partnerships?

Where does the anxiety of abandonment come from?

As children, individuals might experience real losses, denials, or traumas that create them to feel troubled and distrusting of the world. These losses, as well as, injuries can be significant, like the death of a liked one, overlook, or psychological and also physical misuse. However, they can also happen at a much subtler level in day-to-day interactions between parents as well as children. To feel safe, youngsters have to feel safe, seen, as well as soothed when they're distressed. Nevertheless, it's been said that even the most effective of moms and dads are just totally attuned to the children, around 30% of their time. Exploring their basic attachment patterns can use people's insight into their concerns around abandonment as well as denial. Recognizing how their moms and dads connected to them and also whether they experienced a safe accessory versus an insecure one, can provide people hints right into just how they check out connections in the present.

Secure add-ons form when caretakers are regularly offered as well as in harmony with a child's demands. However, ruptures in these new relationships can lead children to build unconfident add-ons. From infancy, individuals find out to act in manner ins which will best get their requirements fulfilled by their moms and dads or caretakers. A mom and dad that might at one moment be present and satisfying the kid's needs, after that at another moment be completely inaccessible as well as denying or, on the opposite end, intrusive and "emotionally starving" can lead the kid to form an ambivalent/ anxious add-on pattern. Kids who experience this kind of add-on tend to feel troubled. They may hold on to the moms and dad in an initiative to obtain their demands satisfied. However, they might additionally have a hard time to feel calmed by the moms and dad. They are typically nervous as well as not sure regarding the moms and dad, who is erratic in their actions, sometimes available as well as caring, as well as various other times, turning down or intrusive in ways that frustrate the child.

How can we overcome the worry of desertion and also change our add-on patterns?

Thankfully, an individual's style or add-on is not repaired. We can create gained safe and secure attachment as adults in numerous ways. As Dr. Lisa, who recently co-taught the on-line program Making Sense of Your Life: Comprehending Your Past to Liberate Your Present as well as Empower Your Future with Dr. Daniel Siegel, has said, "What's barged in a connection can commonly be taken care of in a connection." What she suggests by this is not that a person's present companion can be anticipated to fill the voids or heal all injuries from one's youth, but that experiencing a safe and secure add-on can offer somebody a brand-new model for connections and also how individuals behave in them. If an individual can develop a relationship with somebody that has a lengthy background of being firmly affixed, that individual can learn that she or he doesn't need to frantically cling to a person to get his or her demands met. One more means for people to create more security within themselves is via treatment. Experiencing a safe partnership with a specialist can aid a person kind of gained secure attachment.

Attachment research has better shown that it's not merely what occurs to individuals in childhood that affects their adult connections; it's how much they make sense of and feel the full discomfort of what took place to them. As human beings, we are not helpless sufferers of our past, but we do require to encounter our history to develop a far better future. One of the most effective methods for a person to establish a secure accessory is by making sense of his or her tale. Dr. Daniel Siegel speaks about the value of developing a systematic narrative in aiding people who feel extra secure and reinforced within themselves.

When individuals understand their past, they might be less likely to feel such extreme, knee-jerk fear of abandonment. Nevertheless, even when they do feel worried, they are far much better able to calm themselves down. They can recognize where their concern originates from as well as where it belongs, as well as they can act that is extra sensible as well as appropriate to the truth of their present lives. They can enhance and also reinforce their relationships instead of responding with concern and insecurity as well as developing the distance they so fear.

How To Stay Strong And Positive In Relationship

1. Assess your beliefs about yourself, relationship, world, and what you wish for in life honestly. Do you believe like "Nothing works for me," "Men (or women) always hurt me" or "The world is a hideous place?"If your words sound like some of the ones above, you think bad.

2. Take control of your negative ideas. Let us use the instance, "Nothing works for me" that feels heavy, definitive and permanent. Adjust this idea internally to create room to figure out stuff for you and to appreciate all that has done well for you. Talk about your memories and note that life has gone well for you many times. Try various positive thoughts and see what feels right. For example, "I am open

to meaningful interaction in my life and love." "I am thankful for   "or "I can manage my life."

3. Rewire your brain. Recognize and transform a negative thought or beliefs into one of the most positive thoughts you have developed. This is an unbelievably important change in your mind, so it takes time, energy and persistence to get the idea you want in a safer, new way. However, once you constantly correct it, you will see that your negative thoughts dissipate and healthier ones arise. This is how you take down the negative lens and look at the world more honestly and with more hope.

4. **Always remember that taking care of your expectations are important to your relationship's success.** Discrepancies and conflicts are inevitable in the world of relations, so remember that it's natural and all right. The most important thing is how you and your partner manage and develop in difficult times.

5. **-Remember your partner is also a person.** Not all your partner does is "right" or "good," but you resist the urge to change your critical lens when you are frustrated. Communicate on your desires and don't try to generalize the entire relationship for a moment when you feel hurt.

6. **-Consider the partner deliberately in a positive light.** Thank you for the little things and compassion that your partner shows. Say thank you. Say thank you. It perpetuates a cycle of optimistic and caring relationships.

7. **-Don't take things personally.** There will be poor dates, difficult conversations and times that can be frustrating at the time. Do not add these experiences to your negative pile–take life lessons instead and imagine yourself moving towards your goals. Engage yourself to be happy on your journey to marriage.

How To Stay Away From Negative Thoughts

There are all kinds of things that can ruin an entirely good relationship. Cheating and incompatibility, for example, are two major issues. According to experts, there is one thing that can more than anything else ruin a relationship.

The biggest killer of the relationship can be negative thoughts, "says Bustle, licensed psychologist Nicole Issa, Psy. D. "There is a very close feedback link between the emotions, feelings, and actions. Having negative thoughts will take you down the rabbit hole." It is important to know from Dr. Issa that your thinking habits will contribute to important problems with your relationships. For example, early childhood encounters with your parents can make you feel unworthy of love. That is why you may get into all relationships believing that at some stage, your partner is about to abandon you, and you may be afraid to speak up.

"The truth is that we are making our own reality," Joann Cohen, matchmaker and dating coach, says to Bustle. "If we believe we have a good relationship, we work through things that believe that things are always ok. But when you come to relationships with a negative thought, you always expect the worst not only for your partner but also for the outcome of your relationship." It is important for you to find ways to make them positive in order to prevent negative thoughts. Listed below are some things you can do to remain strong and stop toxic ideas, according to experts, sabotaging your relationship.

1. Think about the first time you have fallen in love with your Spouse

When you pass a rough patch, it is easy to let that cloud judge you. Talk about the "real" feelings of your partner when you start invading your mind, the first time you fell in love with them, and talk about how you felt. "Shutting your eyes and seeing the bright eye person with whom you fell in love will make things look much more positive and doable," says Cohen. At times, we need only a little reminder of the good times to resolve the poor.

2. Letting Go of the Past

To be honest, letting go of the past is absolutely easier said than done. To be fair, "We all have a piece of our history with us to' shield' us against getting hurt again," says Cohen. "And if you continue to bring your old relations and harm to your new relationship, then you sabotage and create the truth that things just do not or will not work." Then, try to separate your past from your present, to prevent your past from creating toxic thoughts. No matter how much they look, speak, or behave the same, your ex isn't your current partner. If you can separate your previous relationship from your new one, being more involved is much easier for you.

3. Find other ways to channel your energy

Toxic thinking will cause you to do unreasonable, relationship-sabotage stuff like hack into your partner's phone or sabotage. To counter this phenomenon, Dr. Issa says that he knows what your thoughts are doing. For instance, why do you feel you need to just "check-in" your partner 20 times in a row? You would also want some affirmation or confirmation that your partner really cares. "Once you know that you have an ability to do (these) stuff, take some time to practice those skills to help you like to count to ten and relax," she says. Find ways to reduce the intense feelings you have so that you will not act in ways that you will regret later.

4. Do not Assume you Know What Your Partner Is Thinking

Negative thoughts are more often than not based on perceptions that do not always exist. "If we put our negative feelings on somebody else or place them on your significant another person, the anger of the other person is what you are reading," Cohen says. The important thing here is never to presume. Do not jump to conclusions. Jump to conclusions. Don't cook it yourself if you can't help it. Get to the edge and chat with your friend. "Try or ask for clarification, take the words on face value," she says. "You never believe you know how they feel."

5. Have That One Person You go-to to Vent Your anger

If you are mad about your partner, it's not uncommon to put all your problems to anyone who's listening. If you are mad about your partner. But, according to Cohen, "When you do that, you create a gap between your meaningful other person and your world, creating more negativity than you know." If you have to really lower yourself down, choose one person, and stay with them. "Saying to everyone is not helpful to your ugly business and will only encourage more negative feelings," she says.

6. Create A List Of Your Toxic Thoughts And Come Up With Positive Ones

Preventing toxic thoughts from destruction takes some self-reflection with constructive alternatives. One of the best things to do while reflecting is to physically write out all the typical ideas that lead to struggles or even divisions. Take it a step further and write a hard proof for or against any thought. After that, come up with a more concise and adaptive alternative thinking. For instance, if you think your partner is no longer interested in you because they didn't reply to your text, please list all other things they could do. "Think about other occasions they have taken a while to answer or to show that they're still involved," says Dr. Issa. "Here the alternative thought may be as simple as' just as I haven't heard of them yet it doesn't mean they don't care.'" Then, the more detailed you are, the more effective it will be.

7. Take Breaking-up Totally Off The Table

Whatever the toxic thoughts are, usually, they are from the same location — fear. In particular, the fear that your partner will leave.

"I use the analogy, you' burn the ship' when you comment," Cohen says. "There is no way to get out of the island when you burn the ship, so work together to survive." If there is no solution, you start seeing what is good in a situation. When you take the chance to break the equation (that is "burning the ship"), you can support your relationship from a place of love and not fear. If your words and actions come from a place of affection, it's much easier for you to remain positive.

Thinking is only a thought at the end of the day. It's not necessarily the truth. If you don't let your relationship consume you, it will improve your relationship.

Role Of Communication In Removing Negative Thoughts

Self-disclosure is a communication skill that allows us to open ourselves to others. For some people, the thought of sharing personal information can be intimidating. We often have the perception that if we open ourselves to others, we will become vulnerable. Self-disclosure leaves us with unpleasant thoughts that are product of our insecurities.

"What if he leaves me when he gets to know the real me?" or "If he learns the truth about me, he will not love me anymore."

Feeling vulnerable in front of your partner is essential, however, make sure he or she is understanding towards your feelings. There are various behaviors that can trigger your insecurities, and you should seek to avoid them. There is also no need to be open towards absolutely everyone, only a select few. Keep in mind that trust is vital to a functional relationship, therefore both you and your partner should develop a bond of trust before openly sharing with one another. In addition, you need to find a balance between the information that you share with everyone, and that which you share only with your partner.

If you are constantly hiding behind a false image, you will never be able to achieve closeness with anyone; you are denying yourself a connection with your partner. There is no such thing as permanently removing triggers of insecurity. You need to learn how to manage them and being able to self-disclose might just be perfect manager of certain triggers.

When it comes to communication, self-disclosure is not only about words. Humans are capable of revealing information about themselves through facial expressions, body language, or our behavior. Some of these you are fully aware of and can control. Some you don't even notice, but others will. The trick is to be aware when and what is appropriate to communicate when insecurity triggers.

We could say we all have two parts: the **open self**, which is the image of your true self that you're comfortable with sharing, and the **hidden self**, the part you're uncomfortable sharing. What you need to do is tap into your **hidden self** and communicate about it to others. In other words, try to expand your **open self** and include to it some part of your **hidden self**. Your relationship can only benefit if you are able to disclose your feelings, thoughts, and needs… and your partner will appreciate your willingness to share.

Chapter 4: How Your Attachment Style Impacts Your Relationship

An attachment style is something that develops when you are a child. Depending on how you are raised, you can either have a healthy sense of how to bond with someone or you might feel that you constantly need to receive reassurance to know that you are cared for. This is definitely something that can end up being projected as you reach adulthood and get into serious relationships. Even though these decisions were made by your parents, they will impact you for the rest of your life.

If your parents were cold and withheld affection, you might have developed a habit of hiding your emotions and needs. Babies who are left to cry for extended periods of time learn how to self-soothe. This can be a difficult process, as they are taught that no one is going to come for them when they are in need. As translated into adulthood, you might feel this way about your partner or you might even believe that your feelings are not important.

Having an anxious attachment means that you are living in fear that your partner could leave you at any moment. These abandonment issues usually stem from having a parent do the same thing during childhood. Children who come from broken homes can often grow to believe that every person in their life is not permanent. If you feel this way, you are never going to feel secure with your spouse because you will be constantly waiting for them to abandon you.

Alternatively, there is an avoidant attachment style. This occurs when you are the one who keeps your partner at a distance, not revealing too many feelings or providing reassurance. This attachment style can make you appear to be cold or not as invested in the relationship, even when you want to be. No matter what kind of attachment style you have, if it is unhealthy and impacting your relationship, therapy will become very beneficial to you. Being able to sort through your issues and understand why you feel this way will provide you with clarity.

45

Chapter 5: Conflict In Relationships

When you are in a serious relationship with another person, you are going to have different opinions frequently. The way that you handle these opinions will showcase the health of your relationships. Not all conflicts are bad, and not all conflicts stem from anxiety. There are plenty of cases when conflict can be healthy. It can show you both differing opinions on the same topic, causing you to re-think your stance on the issue. Even if you do not change your opinion, you should be willing to listen to one another in a respectful way. Those who do not listen to one another tend to engage in conflicts more frequently. These are the kind that can become a burden to any relationship.

This chapter is going to take a look at some of the most common reasons for experiencing conflict in a serious relationship. If you can relate to any of these reasons, then you can consider this the first step toward identifying your problems. As a couple, you should be able to communicate through any problem that you encounter. You do not need to engage in a fight or an argument just because you have differing opinions on a topic. Try your best to remain open-minded, treating your partner the way you wish to be treated. Allow them to express themselves without interrupting them or interjecting with your own opinion. Once you have both had the chance to speak, you should then be able to analyze each side and come to an agreement.

Conflict resolution isn't always going to be direct or simple, but as a healthy couple, you should be able to move past your differences to come to an agreement. When you both want a positive outcome, you are both going to be working toward finding a solution. Those that just want to hash it out are often left disappointed or with unresolved feelings. Both of these feelings can prove to be negative when you suppress them, only to return to them during a later conflict that you encounter. These issues can build up in a very unhealthy way if they are not dealt with properly.

Religion

A topic that often comes with strong opinions, couples can definitely start conflicts over religious beliefs. Whether one of you is religious and the other is not, or you and your partner practice religions, there is a chance that this issue can get brought up during an argument. A lot of the time, issues with religion can be tied to how you plan on raising your children or how your family plays a role in your life.

Understandably, having disagreements about religion can lead to some very tense situations. No matter what you or your spouse believes in, both of you must have respect for one another's beliefs. Any healthy relationship comes with a sense of understanding for each other. If you are intolerant of your partner, then you are contributing to the problem of having conflicts. You need to be able to look at your partner's views as valid, just as you see your own views. Taking an intolerant stance becomes very unhealthy for a long-term relationship, often causing unfixable damage.

Behavior

The way that you behave sends your spouse a very clear message. Even if you are not doing anything that you feel directly impacts your marriage, your actions will speak louder than words. If you cannot do something in front of your spouse, then you should not be doing it when your spouse isn't present. Much like violating the unwritten rules that you have in place, violating certain behavioral patterns can feel just like a betrayal. This will definitely lead to more conflicts and disagreements.

Know that you shouldn't feel controlled by your spouse or vice versa. As long as you both have mutual respect for one another, you should each understand how to act in a way that honors your marriage. This is a tricky balance to find, even for those who have been together for a while. Keep in mind that feelings can also change over the years. The best thing to do is to speak up if your spouse does something that upsets you. This will make it clear as to what you did not care for. Together, you can work on these things.

Dominance

There are typically roles that are taken in any relationship. Usually, one partner takes a more dominant approach, while the other takes on a submissive role. It would be unfair to assume that either one of you **has** to take on these roles, though. The healthiest relationships have a shared sense of dominance. When only one person is dominant, this places the other person at risk of being controlled while in the relationship. Dominance can appear in the form of who takes care of the household and who makes the decisions. It makes sense that a couple should share these duties, even when one of them typically takes on the role themselves.

There is nothing wrong with settling into these roles, but having the flexibility to do things differently is a sign of a healthy relationship. You will realize that there are dominance issues when one of you protests a change in roles. If this makes you feel lesser than or insignificant, then you are likely in need of some work toward your self-esteem. Understand that dominance does not have to be set in stone. Use your own strengths to your advantage by stepping up when you know that it would be beneficial.

Unwritten Rules

Every couple has a set of "rules" in place whether they realize it or not. For example, you should know that if you behave a certain way, this is going to upset your spouse. When you cross these boundaries, not only are you going to upset your partner, but you are going to create a rift in your trust. Betrayal is one of the worst feelings to face, especially from the person who is never supposed to betray you. It can be difficult to create these boundaries when they aren't frequently discussed.

To ensure that you are being fair to your partner, you need to vocalize the things that you are not okay with. This takes away the guesswork and defines a clear line between what you find acceptable and unacceptable. Encourage your partner to do the same thing with you. You might feel that these are things your spouse should already know automatically, but if their actions suggest they do not, you need to tell them. It is healthy for couples to redefine their boundaries, no matter how long they've been married.

Child Bearing

Planning a family is a huge decision to be made by a couple. It comes along with a lot of pressure and being on the same page is essential. Each of you might have your own opinions and preferences when it comes to how many children you would like to have and how you plan on raising them. If you cannot come to an agreement on these decisions, conflict is definitely going to arise. You need to make sure that you are able to compromise when you disagree.

The birth of a child can also come along with many stressors that will test your limits as a couple. When you are both feeling fatigued and overworked, this opens the door for arguments to occur. If you are not careful, you will become very critical of one another. There is also the possibility of becoming stressed out by your lack of finances. Raising a child isn't cheap and if you have not planned adequately, you will struggle. It is very important that you talk to your partner in a realistic way about how you plan on bringing a child into the world.

Work-Related Stress

No matter what you do for a living, there will be times when your job is going to stress you out. Being able to keep your work life and your personal life balanced is very important. Your partner should be someone that you can vent to about work without taking your frustrations out on them. Your behavior can become unhealthy very quickly if you realize that you are in a bad mood and are treating your spouse differently because of something that happened at work. It is unfair to subject your partner to this kind of treatment.

Know that when you leave work, you need to try to keep the problems that you cannot control at work. If you bring these worries and stressors home with you, they are bound to appear in your personal life. Overworking is another thing that tends to drive couples apart. If you are too career-oriented, you are going to be lacking in your marriage. Your partner should be someone who will support you and your goals, yet you need to realize that the stress that you encounter during this time is to no fault of your spouse.

Poor Communication

Being able to talk to your spouse is important, but making sure that you respect and understand one another is critical. So often, couples feel that they have great communication skills, yet they are still driven apart by disagreements. Remember, talking is only one-half of your communication skills. The other half comes from your listening abilities. Be an active listener at all times. If you are distracted or unwilling to listen, you are not going to see the bigger picture.

If you ever get into a disagreement, you can test your communication skills by how quickly you are able to end it. Those who have poor communication will raise their voices, insult one another, and even bring up past issues that should have already been resolved. This is why you should always aim to work on your problems immediately. If you wait, you will begin to suppress them. While you won't always agree on everything, you do need to know that there are boundaries that should not be crossed. Having respect for one another will keep you both in line.

Values

As mentioned above, the things that are most important to you are the things that you value most. There are no right or wrong answers when it comes to these topics. Just as you have your own reasons for why you value what you do, so does your spouse. When these values are not aligned or understood, this opens the door for conflict. This kind of conflict can create difficulties because you will both potentially become stubborn as you try to fight for your cause.

Much like your perception, you need to be able to hear one another out on why you value the things that you do. Try to come from a place of understanding rather than a place of judgment. If you find that your core values do not match, you need to evaluate your relationship to see if you can come to a middle ground. Intolerance is only going to promote unhealthy behaviors and lead to more fighting. Talk about big topics, such as your lifestyle, responsibilities, and religions.

Perception

You and your partner might see the exact same situation differently, and that is normal. While you are a couple, you also need to remember that you are two separate individuals. Your opinions are going to differ. What you need to do is make sure that you understand where your spouse stands on the topics that matter to you. Part of love is being able to accept one another for who you are, not attempting to change your partner so that their views align exactly with your own. There is a fine line between compatibility and control.

As a general rule of thumb, you should openly discuss the things that you value most. If you find that you and your partner see things differently, try to understand their perspective instead of trying to change their mind. This is going to open dialog rather than a disagreement. You might even find that you will be able to understand them better. This kind of mutual respect is very healthy for a relationship, and it shows that you can still love one another, even if you see certain things differently.

Materialistic Difficulties

Even if you do not consider yourself a materialistic individual, your material possessions can drive you apart from your spouse. After you get married, most of your material items are shared. There can be a sense of competitiveness that arises when you realize that one of you is contributing more than the other. Alternatively, you might be tempted to compare what you have to what other couples have. Know that your lifestyle and relationship is unique; your success is not dependent on these material possessions.

If you find that your arguments are stemming from what you both have as a couple, you will realize that too much focus is being placed on material items. You can try to get back to what you love about being together, minus these possessions. Think about why you fell in love with your spouse in the first place. If you didn't have anything except for each other, you would appreciate one another for the qualities that you each possess instead of the items that you can procure. Conflicts can become very messy when you realize that you are simply fighting over things that are temporary.

Chapter 6: The Life Cycle Of Relationships

Relationships tend to go through five levels – some are more satisfying than others. So if you and your partner are able to work together with each stage as they arrive, the incentives will be combined with development and a stronger relationship. However get caught in one of these stages, and you and your better half could simply wind up attempting to give up.

Falling in love

Also called the "fixation period." it is the most glamorized period of the cycle of marriage. It's something that happens in the movies, and it's something that any of us care about!

After a time of growing up, our passion deepens and becomes relaxed with each other. Finally, we have a closer connection with our partner; we feel protected and treasured. A lot of people misinterpret that as the highest degree of affection we should have got, but they'd be mistaken.

Infatuated drug-love wears off – campbell extends this wear-off from two months to two years – depending on the pair. Deepened passion continues a time after that, until the 3-4-year point of a relationship. Yet instead we're going to reach the risk zone.

The reality check

This is better known as "the love hangover" or "the disillusionment period." according to dr. Campbell, an incredibly large number of marriages are taking place at this time. At this point, we begin to reflect on our weaknesses and shortcomings, rather than on the ways we are. The passion we have can be replaced by frustration and anger.

We can continue to get irritated with the little stuff more often than not. We will feel less cared about or loved than we used to do. Before this point, it was all right (though difficult to be parted) to let each other concentrate on work tasks – now, choosing work over each other feels like negligence.

At this point, we sometimes make the error of attempting to "transform" our partners by punishment: disagreement, violent conduct, and emotional isolation...the list goes on.

How can you work your way through this tough patch successfully? This stage is a time to reflect on your interactions – most importantly on the ability to settle disputes (see this post on how to argue effectively). Campbell's tips for getting through this point include:

• Acknowledging and appreciating your similarities

• Sharing control and knowing dominance won't get you what you want

• Recognizing that peace without conflict doesn't happen

• Embracing life because it is now time to remind yourself of your own personal shortcomings and failures, and to reflect on how your spouse makes up for them. Know what makes a team of you!

If you can't settle your differences successfully at this point, you can find yourself coming back to it regularly in your relationship. Some people have been trapped in this stage for years – never hitting the next point – until they stopped calling.

Stability

You've actually worked out how to compromise with – and not fight – your friend. Congratulations, you've made a hell of the past relationship, and passion is back! Phase one's older, smarter brother is the stabilization stage. At this point, you've embraced each other for who you are, and you don't want to change them anymore (you've never been able to do that anyway).

You have strong boundaries for each other at this point, as well as reciprocal respect. This love is true; it lasts. Today, with more faith than ever before, you can tell that you love each other completely for who you are.

Even in moments of disagreement or immaturity, it is understood that hurtful conduct is not due to either of you being cruel or uncaring. Yes, at times, you could struggle and have your differences. Yet this doesn't preclude you from maintaining a close bond with them.

At this point, however, some couples end their relationships. Stability can make certain people feel nervous or bored. Although it's normal to skip the thrilling infatuation of stage 1, some people are beginning to wonder if they can get that back with a new boyfriend. It may be the ignition that would set off an extramarital affair. Our advice, huh? Weigh what you've got to earn against what you've got to lose. Though falling in love can be fun and thrilling, it doesn't last forever.

Commitment

At the point when you're intending to get hitched, this is the stage you're going to need to be in before you pose an inquiry. Couples now understand that while they needn't bother with one another (speedy updates that people will truly exist all alone), they need to be with one another, deficiencies or not.

Some people don't skip stage one; the only other way to get back to that is to meet someone new to marry, so they don't want anything else except their partner. Commitment is a real symbol of long-lasting devotion.

Happiness

In the happiness point, people step past the inner workings of their partnership – they've got all packed up by now – and out into the world around them. Such couples prefer to collaborate on projects together. To certain couples, it means launching a company or a charity together. For some, this stage involves working together to grow up and sustain a family. Among these purposes, this period is most sometimes referred to as the period of co-creation.

Couples seem to spend a number of years at this point. Yet it's always important to note to carry on sustaining your relationship while spending this time and energy in their new passions!

Please note, these steps are not sequential, so happiness is not always an end goal. Numerous individuals experience these periods a few times in their relationships, months or years one after another.

This is crucial to have the option to perceive the phase at which you and your partner are in, so you can settle on more advantageous choices on whether to improve your relationship, instead of making somebody stage debilitate or fall apart.

Chapter 7: Love And Relationship - Advice For Couples

Advice for couples

1. And at those times when you fail to like each other, choose to love one another. Love is a engagement, not a emotion.

2. When your husband / wife is calling, always answer the phone: Try to hold your phone off while you are with your partner where possible.

3. Make time a priority together: Schedule a clear night date. Time is the "relationship money" so spend time regularly in your marriage.

4. Surround yourself with friends who are going to strengthen your marriage: get rid of people who may tempt you to compromise your character.

5. Make humor your marriage's soundtrack: share moments of joy. And finding reasons to joke even in the hard times.

6. Note that there isn't going to be a "winner" and a "loser" in any debate. You're partners in this and you'll either win or lose together. Join forces to find a solution.

7. Realize that a strong marriage never has two strong people at the same time: in the times where the other feels vulnerable, it is usually a husband and wife who ends up being strong for each other.

8. Prioritize what's happening in the bedroom: Building a strong marriage takes more than sex, but building a strong marriage without it is almost impossible. 9. Note that marriage is not 50/ 50 — divorce is 50/ 50: it must be 100/ 100 for marriage. This doesn't

split everything in half, but both partners do give everything they have.

10. Give each other your best, not your leftovers after you have put the best on each other.

11. Learn from others but don't feel the need to equate your life or marriage to that of someone else. The plan of God for your life is majestically special.

12. Don't put your marriage on hold while you raise your children or you will end up with an empty nest and an unhappy family.

13. Never keep secrets from one another: This is some of the best advice I can give you on marriage. Since secrecy is the enemy of intimacy.

14. Never lie to one another: Lies destroy faith and trust is the basis for a healthy marriage.

16. Give them your forgiveness immediately when your husband / wife violates your faith: It will encourage healing and provide the ability to restore faith. You have to be able to say, "I love you. I forgive you. Let's move on."

17. Be cooperative with each other: It is often more important for your partner than your schedule.

18. Model the form of marriage your sons want to grow up as good husbands and your daughters want to grow up as good wives.

20. Never speak poorly to other people about your spouse or vent them online: Protect your spouse at all times and everywhere.

21. Still wear your wedding ring: it shows you that you are still related to your partner and shows the rest of the world that you are out of boundaries.

22. Associate with a religious community: A strong church will make a difference in your marriage and health.

23. Pray together: In the midst of it, every union with Christ is better.

24. When you have to choose between saying nothing or asking your partner something important, say nothing every time.

25. Never see divorce as an option: note that a "perfect union" is just a couple of imperfect people who refuse to give up.

Things successful couples do that help them stay together.

1. They don't take each other for granted Happy couples show each other their gratitude every chance they get. We don't take each other for granted and we know that each day is a blessing to be shared with their partner.

2. We are kind to one another Couples who have relationships that are kind to one another. Even though angry they prefer goodness. An dispute does not turn into a shouting match in which every person wrestles to be right. Alternatively, disputes are seen as chances of understanding.

Consider the good things that your partner does every day. Did they carry out the recycling for example, or come home for dinner early one night? Regardless of how small the gesture is, make it a habit to acknowledge the kindness when it happens and make a mental note of how happy it makes you feel. And mention it to them when you see your friend.

3. We pay attention to each other Successful couples have learned the art of listening and being aware of each other. We know how to overcome disputes by trying to understand the needs of each other, and by making an attempt to satisfy those needs as best we can.

4. They have compassion Successful couples gracefully fix breakdowns in relationships. Those couples pause and iron out their differences with love and concern rather than walking out of the room in a huff or giving the silent treatment. It's not her style to let things "blow over." Rather, they work actively to fix a disturbance to the relationship by letting each other know how they feel and making an attempt to address what doesn't work in the relationship. We respect the feelings of each other and step forward by working about their issues and doing what they can to relieve the emotional pain.

5. They are playful Successful couples, while they are usually happy, it can be difficult to understand ties. Consequently, when appropriate, they know how to spread tension with playfulness and a little humour. One of the main ingredients in their formula for a fruitful relationship is a dose of laughter.

6. Both are devoted couples who share a fulfilling partnership are devoted to each other and their relationship's wellbeing. We plan to stick it out even though things get rough. Most significantly, even though they do not like each other they tend to love each other. Their partnership is paramount.

Meet SOMEONE WITH ANXIETY What you need to learn and do Dating can be incredibly difficult for someone with anxiety disorders or an anxiety disorder. Often it might sound like the discomfort in the relationship is a third party, someone who wriggles in between you and your partner. That person sows doubts and uncertainty constantly. No one has prepared you for this, and you can not pick who you are going to fall for. For dating there is no high school education, far less dating someone with a mental health disorder.

Nonetheless, anxiety should not sever the relationship or place a strain on it to the point that it becomes difficult to enjoy. You will love each other more deeply and communicate in a different way through knowing anxiety in general, and how it affects both your partner and your relationship. Educating yourself will also alleviate tremendous tension.

The book lays down what you need to learn and do while dating someone with anxiety: how to help your partner, consider how your relationship can be influenced by anxiety, search after your own mental health and more. Keep reading if you want to make sure that the tension in your relationship will not become a third party.

The Anxiety Coming Out Talk If you ask for it after months of dating or deduce it, there will be a point where your partner admits they are struggling with anxiety. It's a critical friendship moment, so be polite and don't judge. Thank you for trusting you with this knowledge they most likely didn't share with a lot of people. See it as the starting point of a conversation you might sometimes resurface.

Knowing Anxiety and What It Does To Your Partner

Understanding these simple anxiety facts will help you to better understand and support your partner, anxiety is a real problem, not something made up. It's for mental health.

Anxiety is normal, it's something everybody has. It's only being a issue or disorder if it's serious.

Anxiety can be a crippling disease which prevents people from working and living a normal life.

Anxiety causes people to experience fight-or-flight responses and focus over non-life-threatening problems, like worrying that a spouse will cheat or leave.

Anxiety can't "repair" or "cure."

Most people who have need for anxiety have it not. They worry themselves that their fear is a burden on others.

Despite coping with anxiety, there are millions of people who have successful relationships, and are happy.

Anxiety symptoms may occur regularly in waves, or both. People with anxiety disorders or problems can have periods of time where symptoms don't occur.

Anxiety is not moral, or logical. It causes people to think about something when there is no evidence to indicate that it is worth worrying. This even leads them to behave irrationally, often. It is undoubtedly what your partner knows best.

Anxiety is not an affliction. Anxiety is therapeutic. Psychotherapy will ease the symptoms and teach people how to cope better.

How Anxiety Can Impact Your Relationship

If you encounter people with anxiety, your partner will probably spend a lot of time worrying and ruminating on anything that could go wrong or be wrong with the relationship already. Here are some examples of thoughts and questions which could run through their brain: What if they don't love me as much as I love them?

What if he lies about me?

What if somehow he hides from me?

What if he tricks me?

What if he wants to trick me?

Even if someone else likes him better?

What will happen if my anxiety destroys our relationship? (The anxiety)

What if we split up? What if he's not going to text me back?

And if I'm not the first to reach out?

What if he is spiriting on me?

Most people have some of those nervous feelings, at least. They are a normal part of being in a relationship, especially a new relationship.

Nevertheless, people with anxiety disorders or an anxiety disorder appear to have such nervous thoughts more frequently and more deeply.

"Our minds take over and go right into the worst-case scenario," the nervous thoughts trigger physiological symptoms, including shortness of breath, insomnia and anxiety attacks. Anyone with anxiety can respond with a fight-or-flight response to relationship stress, as if the stress was a physical assault.

Anxious thoughts often encourage your partner to behave in ways that stress you out and strengthen the relationship. For example, people with anxiety often use vulnerable methods to test their partner's commitment. Typically such methods tackle one of their nervous convictions.

Let's say your partner is full of guilt that he's the first to initiate contact. He starts to fear that you don't like him as much as he likes you because you don't send out the first text as much as he does. The fear is intensifying and he starts to feel that if he didn't reach out first you would never speak with him.

To fix the fear, he agrees the ghosting on you for a while is a good idea. That forces you to communicate first. You can reach out to him a couple of times before he feels good at realizing you're going to make the effort. The proof lets him doubt his nervous, unreasonable conviction that you're not going to reach out first. Yet it is clearly not a sound plan.

Unfortunately people experience several anxiety-motivated behaviors in relationships. Here are a few more signs to watch out for: Being frustrated, irritable Being distracted and having difficulty concentrating Coming off as overly critical

Avoidant or passive aggressive actions Dating Someone with Social Anxiety If you are dating someone with social anxiety, the anxiety most definitely would impact your social life. You may not be willing to take your partner to all the social activities or meetings to which you plan to go. This, like other types of anxiety, may lead to disagreements or cause the two of you to broaden apart.

"I felt like I won the jackpot with her. She just seemed to understand what I was going through, and led me through it."

How to Cope With It

Anxiety does not jeopardize the friendship. You can have a healthy relationship and avoid anxiety from causing too much tension using the right coping strategies.

Encouraging Your Partner to Work With a Therapist or Try Couples Therapy

It's tempting to help you while you look after others by pretending to be a substitute therapist. You're not a doctor, the question is. It will be emotionally exhausting to try to play this part. It could make your partner hate you.

You are not liable for your partner's counseling. This is why your friend should be directed to a therapist with gentleness. A therapist may help them develop their way of coping with anxiety, in relationships and outside.

Seek couples therapy if you are in a serious, long-. Many of the questions may be built on your connection.

Your friend will take the burden from meeting with a couple's counselor. You allow them to take part in the therapy rather than encourage them to do it on their own.

Going to Therapy Yourself

You will do so yourself, whether your partner accepts or rejects your request for treatment. It allows you to develop the skills you need to consider and resolve the anxiety of your partner. You can also learn how to support your nervous partner more effectively.

It is easy to think about taking care of yourself when you meet someone with anxiety. You should also reflect on your own mental health by going to therapy.

Chapter 8: Possessiveness - A Hurdle For Relationship

Possessiveness in marriage is the urge to control or dominate every aspect of the life of a spouse.

Steps to Overcome Possessiveness

Have you ever struggled against the emotions of possession and jealousy? These are the two significant factors that can wreak havoc. Yet being mindful of your actions and determined to change is half the battle won! Then you can put these negative emotions aside from the techniques below so that you can experience healthy relationships.

The symptoms of envy

The main features of a jealous person are overwhelming, complicated inferiority, and egotism. While we may know a jealous person is selfish, we may not realize that he has a complex of inferiority. That's because, with a display of self-confidence, he covers it.

Egoism brings back its nasty head when your companion pays even a little interest to somebody or something else instead of you. You feel bitter that you are not the object of attention and that jealousy overcomes you. At such moments, you're not going to think about anyone but your own well-being.

Do you have such feelings? If you do, then you must know that they are jealous.

Check Yourself for Egotism Answer these questions:

- Am I ready to give the gain back?

- Am I willing to grant such a privilege?

If you both have negative responses, you are most likely selfish.

If you are jealous, what you have to do is overcome your feelings of inferiority and the intense need for approval.

Though most people tend to share these terms, jealousy and envy are two different emotions. Envy is when you want to do like the other guy. Jealousy is when you want to be the only one who does well. The jealous person wants to take away the success of the other guy.

Envy can be a useful emotion if you use it properly. You should inspire yourself and your reputation to change.

Possessiveness

There is no other person involved in possessiveness. You don't feel worth it unless someone loves you and proves it by smothering you.

Possession and envy come both from the same source: an overwhelming desire for affection and respect.

The way to change There are strategies you can use to reduce or eliminate these negative feelings if you have these disagreeable characteristics. With some effort, you can be well on your way to fun, competitive, and possessive relationships.

Here are five fantastic tips to help you resolve these sentiments:

Nobody's okay, remember! Everyone has some shortcomings. You don't have to be faulty to help. Why should you allow others to judge your value?

Take care of yourself. Whether you face problems or a breakup in your relationship, note that blame leads to shame and weakness.

Blaming your actions, if possible, but not yourself. Hold away from self-compassion.

Believe you will adjust. Believe it. You may think your envy and pride are an inherent part of your character that you cannot alter. But you can adapt! You only need to remember people who stop smoking or stop drinking alcohol, so they can understand this shift if you can change for the better!

All of them are their own human. Most people in romantic relations feel they "belong" to each other. This is one of the jealous and possessive person's most dangerous beliefs. It doesn't matter how much you gave your lover; you just can't think of them like your house or your car. Let them go if they have decided to leave you. By caging someone who no longer cares about you, there is simply no reason. Such a partnership would not be harmonious.

Have a hobby. Take it up. One who makes another person the focus of his life is a person who is inherently jealous and possessive. One right way to end your life's emphasis on your lover is to become self-interested. Upgrade your hobby skills, and you will find your relationship is no longer a concern. That's because you're going to be excited about something but your lover.

So when you are jealous and possessive, do these tips and improve your sense of self-worth and learn to see things as they really are. As a consequence, relationships will grow into beauty and joy!

Conclusion

This book should be a manual for managing anxiety and anger to improve your relationship.

The next step is to stop reading and start applying the lessons in real life. Do whatever you have identified as necessary to curb anger and ensure the health and wellness of you and the people around you. You will find that many people are still ignorant about the proper ways of anger management. You will realize that the majority of those who seem to have it all together are just suppressing anger, and it will harm them in the end. To that end, try to engage them and teach them a thing or two you have learned herein. You may even recommend or gift this book to them.

The moment you understand the anger, it becomes easier to deal with it. Anger management is essential in everyday life. This book has taken you through the topic of anger management. There is no one specific thing that a person can do to manage anger overnight. However, if you follow the right steps with dedication and commitment, you will get the results you seek. Combine a number of treatment options if need be. If you are working with a therapist, follow all the instructions he/ she gives you and keep an open communication channel.

All the best !